Basic Fishing Lure Carving

Greg Hays

Pro Runner

Schiffer Publishing Ltd

4880 Lower Valley Road, Atglen, PA 19310 USA

Dedication

I dedicate this book to my wife, Debbie, for without her I probably would not have finished it. I also want to give thanks to family and friends for their encouragement.

Other Schiffer Books on Related Subjects

Freshwater Fish Carving, Jim Fliger, $35.00
Carving Fish & Pond Life, Rick Roth, $39.95
Top of the Line Fishing Collectibles, Donna Tonelli, $39.95
Collectible Fishing Reels, Carl Ciati, $29.95
Vintage Fishing Reels of Sweden, Daniel Skupien, $39.95

Copyright © 2006 by Greg Hays
Library of Congress Control Number: 2006926882

Designed by Mark David Bowyer
Type set in Eras Md BT / Eras Bk BT

ISBN: 0-7643-2505-1
Printed in China

Published by Schiffer Publishing Ltd.
4880 Lower Valley Road
Atglen, PA 19310
Phone: (610) 593-1777; Fax: (610) 593-2002
E-mail: Info@schifferbooks.com

For the largest selection of fine reference books on this and related subjects, please visit our web site at
www.schifferbooks.com
We are always looking for people to write books on new and related subjects. If you have an idea for a book please contact us at the above address.

This book may be purchased from the publisher.
Include $3.95 for shipping.
Please try your bookstore first.
You may write for a free catalog.

In Europe, Schiffer books are distributed by
Bushwood Books
6 Marksbury Ave.
Kew Gardens
Surrey TW9 4JF England
Phone: 44 (0) 20 8392-8585; Fax: 44 (0) 20 8392-9876
E-mail: info@bushwoodbooks.co.uk
Website: www.bushwoodbooks.co.uk
Free postage in the U.K., Europe; air mail at cost.

Contents

Introduction

I started carving seriously about twelve years ago. I am a self-taught carver, although I have picked up a few pointers from friends in my carving club and, of course, from the many books that I have purchased over the years. Carving caricatures has always been my favorite thing to carve, but I also carve on hiking sticks and walking canes.

But about a year ago I decided to try my hand at lure carving. Let me tell you this has been the most exciting experience for me. Lure carving is very challenging. I have spent many hours experimenting with different techniques and designs. I love this hobby so much that I decided to write this book, *Carving Fishing Lures.*

In these pages you will find a pattern for a favorite lure and step-by-step directions that will take you from a block of wood to a finished lure. Each step is illustrated with a photograph to help you along the way. You will also find plans for another of my lures that you can carve on your own. I have developed tools that make the carving of lures easier, and I will share with you some jigs and rigs that will help you in your lure building.

Again I just want to say that lure carving is the most fun and the most satisfying hobby. I hope that this book will help and encourage you to become a lure carver too. Good Luck!

Tools & Supplies

The following tools are needed to complete this project:

Table saw
Scroll saw
Power carver with small saw bit
Cylinder-shape diamond bit
Round-nose stone bits
Carving knife

Drill press
1/16" drill bit
3/8" Frostner bit
Hobby vise
Two small Quick-Grip bar clamps
Screwdriver
Round-nose pliers
Latex gloves

Materials

Balsa or basswood for the body:
    1" wide x 1-1/4" tall x 3-1/4" long
Balsa or basswood for the filler:
    1/8" thick x 3/4" wide x 5" long
Clear acrylic sheet: 1" wide x 3/32" thick, x 2" long
0.031 stainless steel wire, 12" long
Devcon 2-ton epoxy
Fast drying spray paint: white, orange, and red

Sandpaper: 80 grit, 400 grit, and 1000 grit
Emery board file
Small flat riffler file
Steel wool: 0000
Paper tape
#4 Treble hooks
Split rings

Jigs & Rigs

The following drawings should help you build the epoxy stand, drill guide block, and paint stand used in this book. These simple structures greatly help in the lure making process.

The Design of the Drill Guide Block

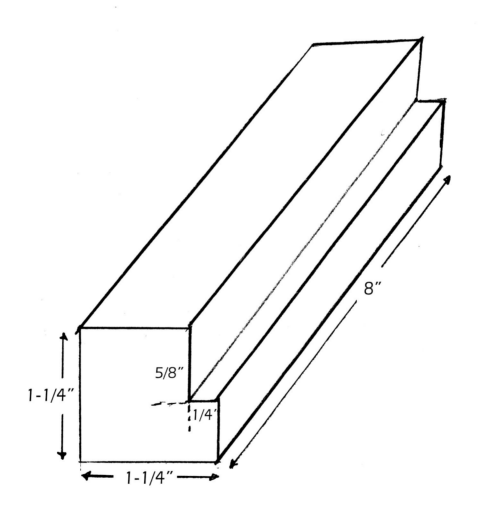

The Epoxy Stand, front view

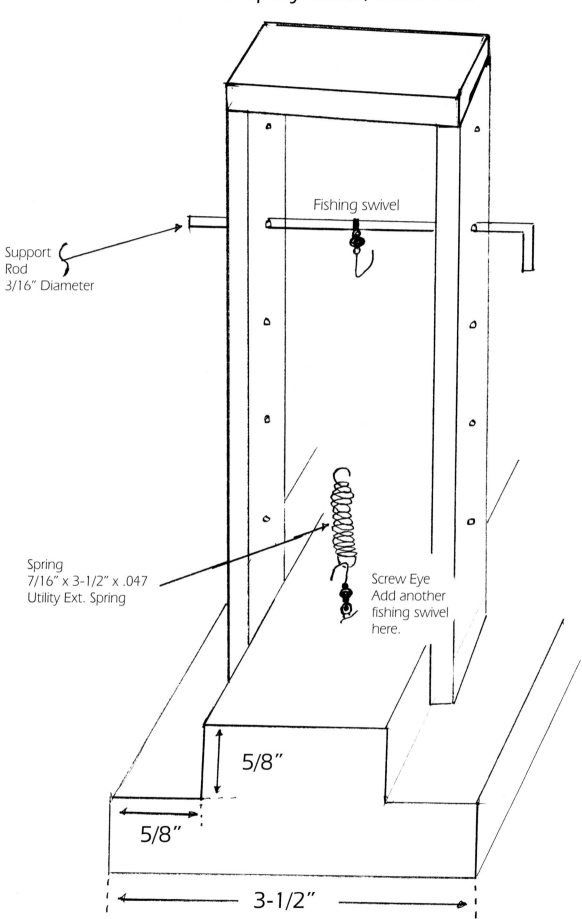

Support
Rod
3/16" Diameter

Fishing swivel

Spring
7/16" x 3-1/2" x .047
Utility Ext. Spring

Screw Eye
Add another
fishing swivel
here.

5/8"

5/8"

3-1/2"

The Epoxy Stand, side view

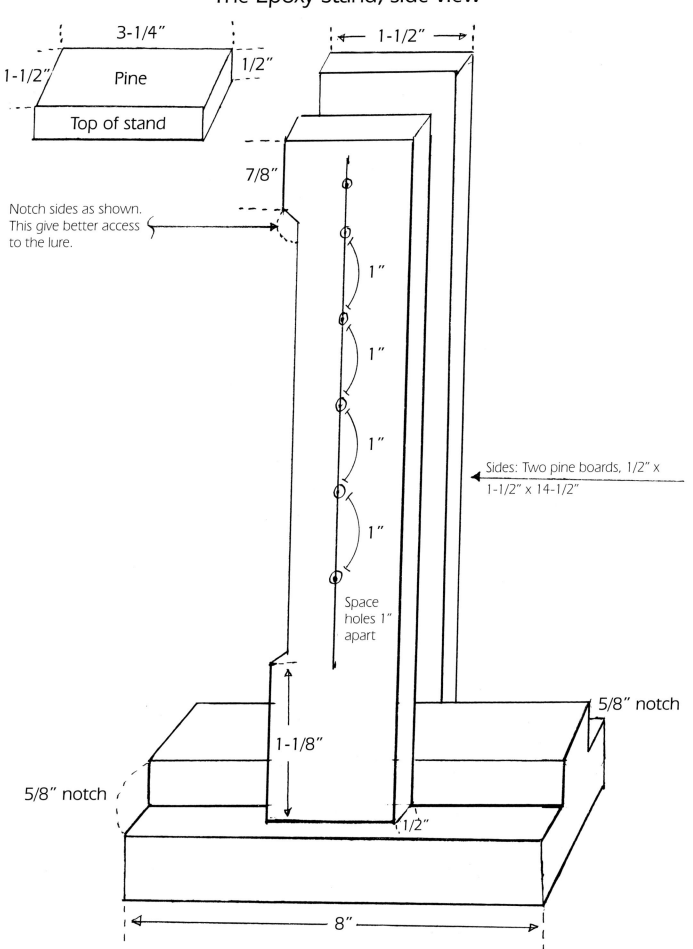

3-1/4"

1-1/2"

Pine

1/2"

Top of stand

1-1/2"

7/8"

Notch sides as shown. This give better access to the lure.

1"

1"

1"

1"

Space holes 1" apart

Sides: Two pine boards, 1/2" x 1-1/2" x 14-1/2"

5/8" notch

1-1/8"

5/8" notch

1/2"

8"

The Paint Stand

Top: 1 x 4 x 25-1/2" pine

Channel

25-1/2"

8 channels, 3/8" x 3/8" x 3-1/2", w/ dado

4 dividers, 1/8" x 3-1/2"
X 10-7/8"
3/16" Diameter

Fishing swivels: 10

Ext. springs: 5
7/16" x 3-1/2" x .047

Slats: 6

3/8" x 1" x 25-5/8"

PAINT

Space shelves as
needed: 1" x 4" x 24"

Sides: 2 pieces,
1" x 4" x 70"

70"

2" x 4" x 24" pine

24"

21"

You will need a horsehair air
conditioning filter, which you
can purchase at your local
hardward store. Cut a piece
11" high x 25-1/2" wide.
Mount the filter to the back
of the paint chamber.

10"

Foot: 2" x 4" pine

12"

Carving the Pro Runner Lure

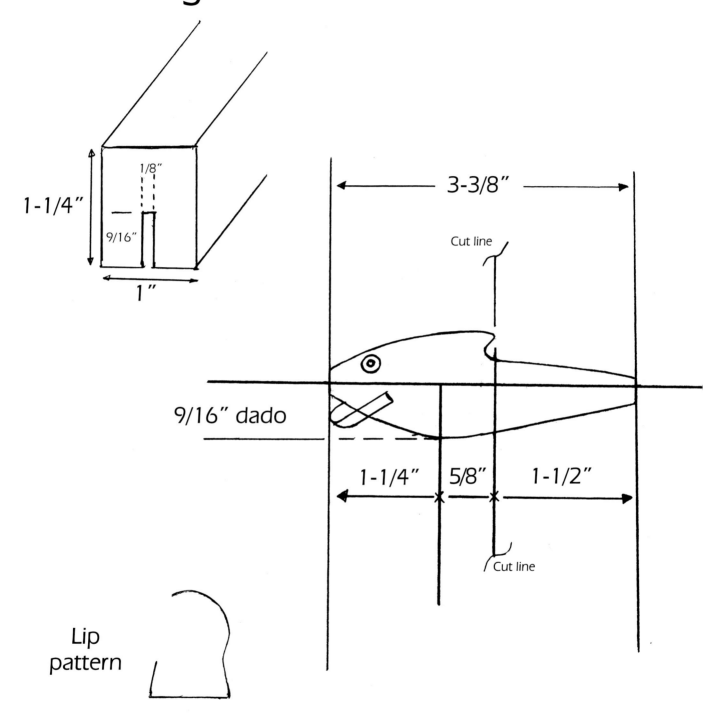

1-1/4"

1/8"

9/16"

1"

3-3/8"

Cut line

9/16" dado

1-1/4" 5/8" 1-1/2"

Cut line

Lip
pattern

The measured drawing for the Pro Runner lure. The lip pattern is placed on 3/32" acrylic. After you have studied the drawing of the Pro Runner lure and feel confident that you understand how Pro Runner is made, it is time to get started. First make yourself a cardboard pattern of Pro Runner. Pick the wood that you are going to use. I use basswood, but you can use balsa or any of the top lure-building woods that you prefer.

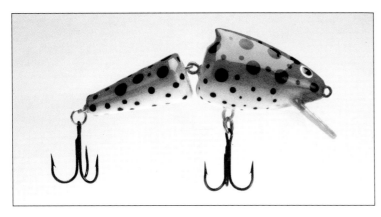

The Pro Runner lure

This is how your blank should look. Okay, let's move on.

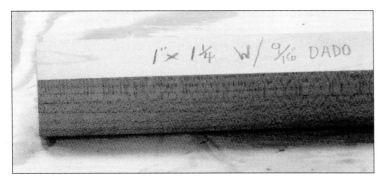

At the table saw cut a blank to match drawing. It should be at least 3-3/8" long and 1" w x 1-1/4" h. If you are going to make several lures just add to the length of the blank.

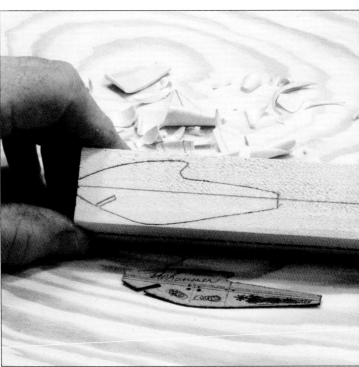

Using the cardboard pattern trace Pro Runner on the blank. Draw in a line down the side of the blank that represents depth of dado cut.

Find the exact center of the blank. Cut a 1/8" dado 9/16" deep all the way down the center of the blank.

Check to make sure the depth of the dado is 9/16" of an inch.

After you have cut the first lure from the blank continue cutting out the lines. Cut just outside the lines, not on or inside the lines, because this could affect the fit of the wire rigging later on. For this step I use a scroll saw.

Cut the first lure from the blank.

When cutting in the lip slot you can cut on inside of the lines. The object here is not to remove too much wood. The acrylic material is 3/32" thick.

I use a scrap piece of acrylic to check the fit while cutting in the lip slot. You are looking for a good snug fit as you can see in the picture. It is now time to move on to the carving.

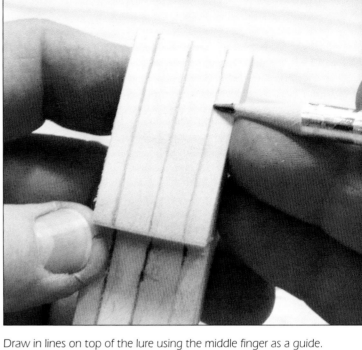

Draw in lines on top of the lure using the middle finger as a guide. Draw a center line down the top of the lure.

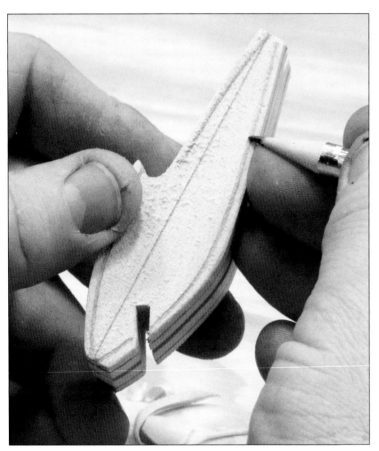

Begin by drawing in some layout lines for carving. Using your middle finger as a guide draw in lines as shown on both sides of the lure.

Continue the lines at the nose of the lure.

This is how Pro Runner should look at this point. We will start by carving to the lines.

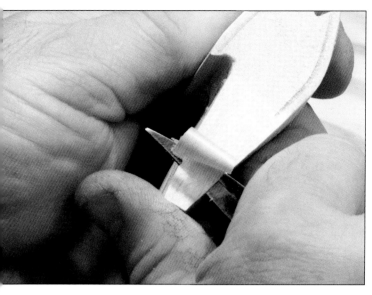

Start at the middle of the lure. Place your knife blade at a slant and cut down to the tail.

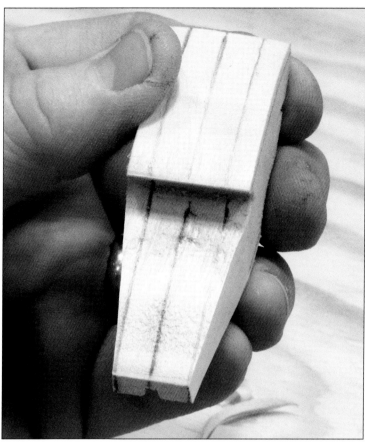

This is what it should look like after tail cuts.

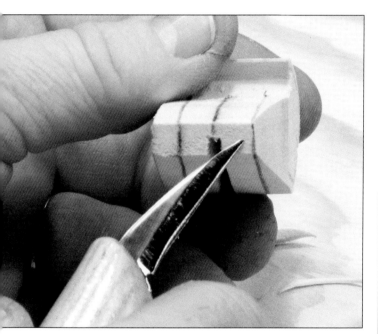

Cut to the reference line on tail of lure. It may take more than one cut, but this is how it should look when it is finished.

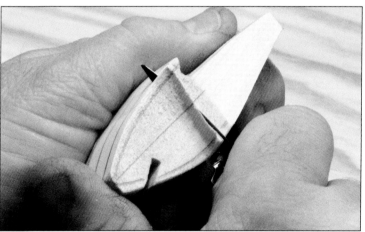

Moving to the nose of the lure we want to do the same thing. Start in the middle of the lure and carve down to the line on the nose. Again do not try to make it in one cut. It may take several cuts.

Do the exact same thing on the other side of the tail.

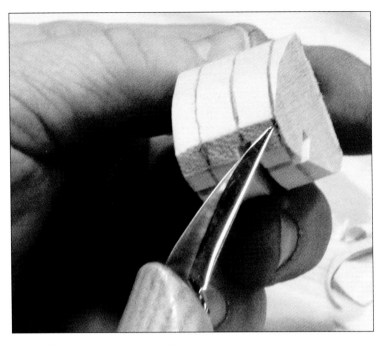

This is how the lure should look after these cuts.

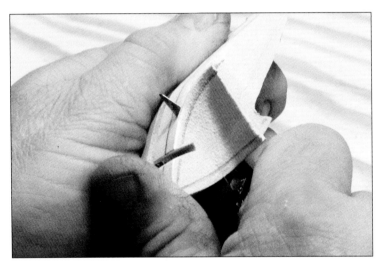

Now do the exact same process on the other side of the nose of the lure.

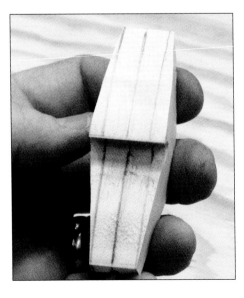

This is how Pro Runner should look up to this point.

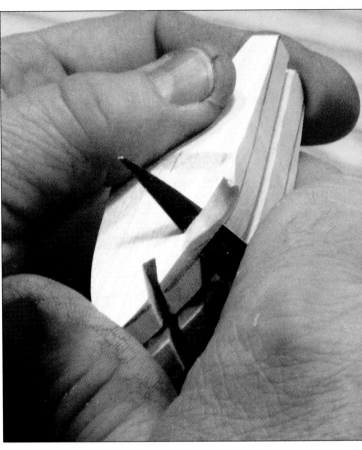

Now it is time to carve the lines on the top and bottom of lure. Start in the middle and carve to the line carrying the cut to the nose of the lure. This creates a beveled edge that tapers down as it reaches the nose and, later, the tail.

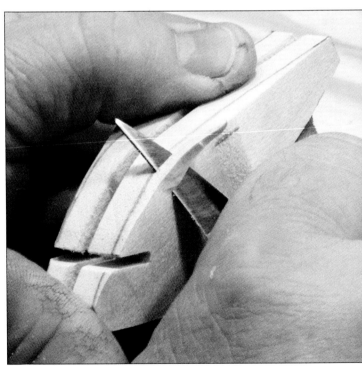

Do the exact same thing on the other side of the nose of the lure.

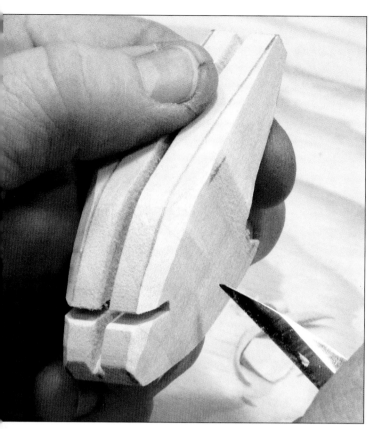

This is how *Pro Runner* should look after making these cuts.

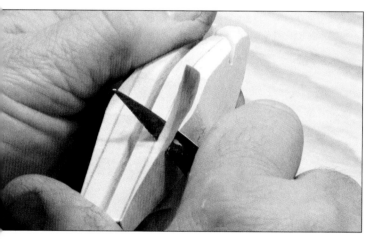

Now carve the tail with the same process.

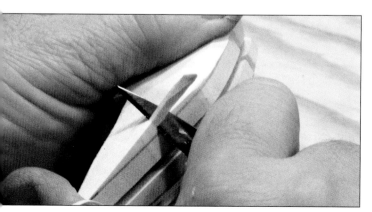

Do the same on the other side of the tail.

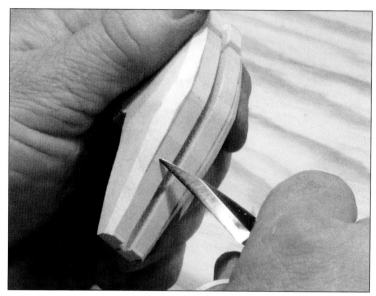

This is how *Pro Runner* should look at this point.

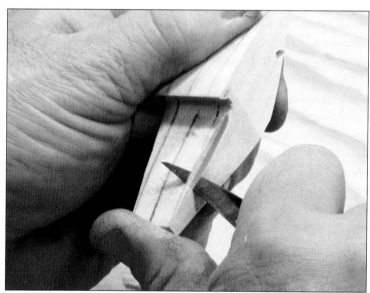

Do the same on the topside of tail.

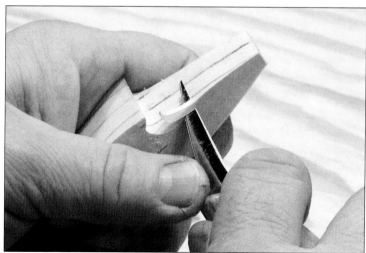

Repeat on each side.

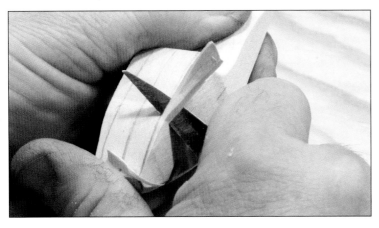

Repeat the same process toward the nose on the top of the lure.

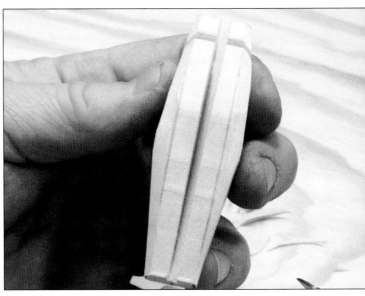

This is how Pro Runner should look from the bottom of the lure.

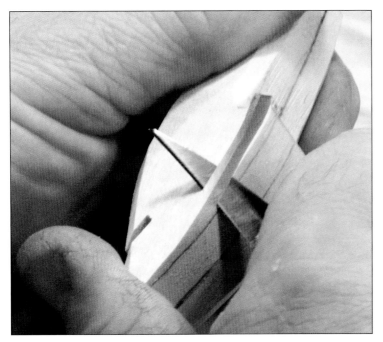

Do the same on the other side.

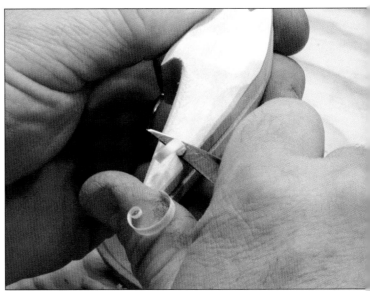

Now that we have carved the basic shape by removing all the guide lines it is time for your true carving skills to kick in. Just remember when you remove wood from one side you must remove wood on the other side. It is important to keep it symmetrical. Okay, let's begin at the tail of the lure. Start at the middle and work your way down to the tail.

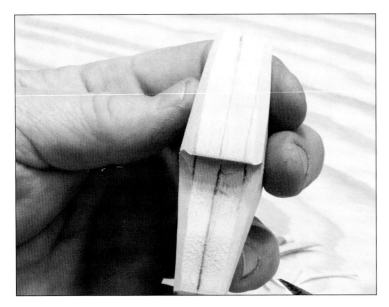

This is how Pro Runner should look from a top view.

Do the same on the other side.

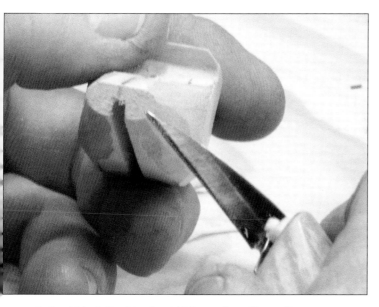

It should look like this after initial rounding of lure tail.

This is how the nose of the lure should look after rounding.

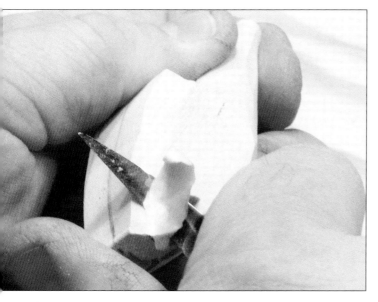

Start rounding the nose of the lure as you did on the tail.

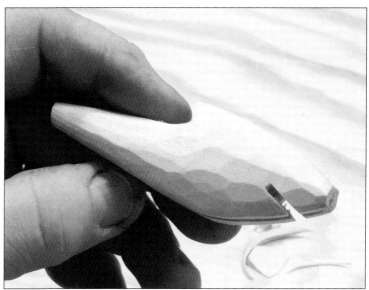

This is how the profile on the right side of the lure should look.

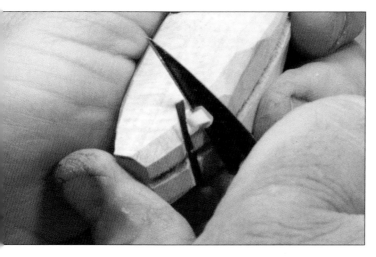

Do the same on both sides of the nose. Remember to keep it symmetrical.

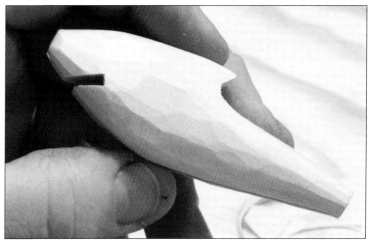

This is how the profile of the lure looks from left side.

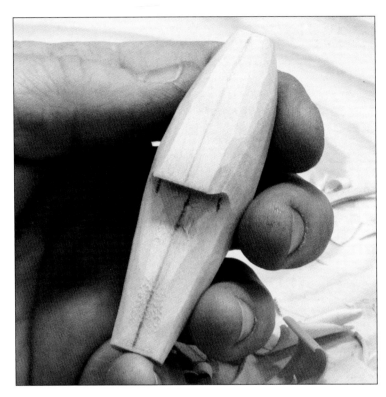

This is how Pro Runner should look from the top at this point.

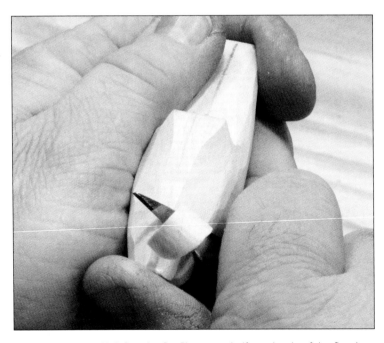

Now we will define the fin. Place your knife at the tip of the fin, slant the blade away from center line and carve all the way to the nose of the lure.

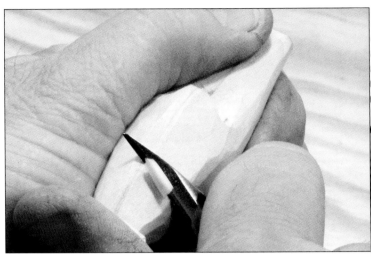

Repeat the same cut. Carve up to the center line of the fin. Repeat these same cuts for other side of lure fin.

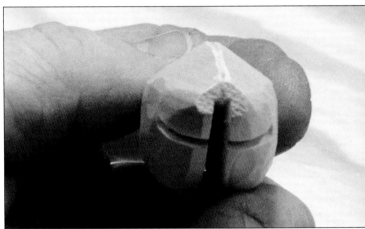

This is how the fin should look at this point.

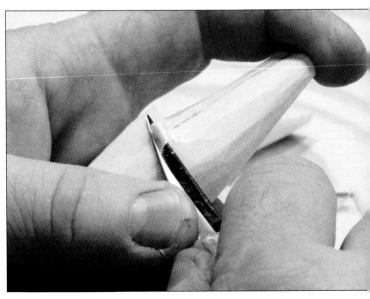

Shape and define the fin.

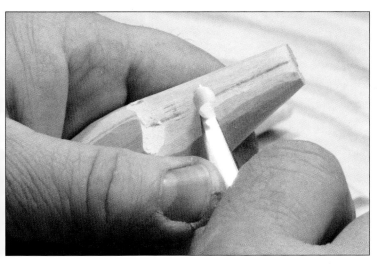

Round and shape the tail. Carve away the guide line on top of the tail.

Pro Runner should look like this at this point.

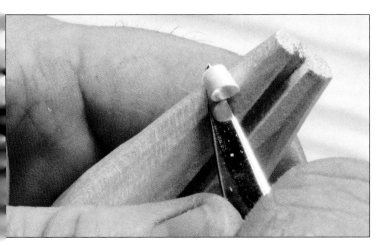

Continue to carve around the tail. Take your time here. The object is to keep it symmetrical and not to remove too much wood.

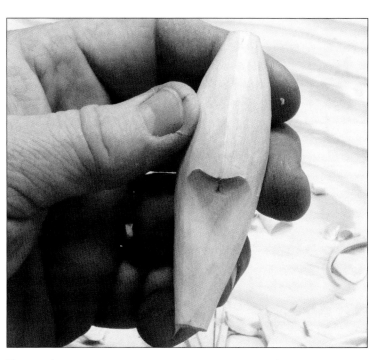

The top view.

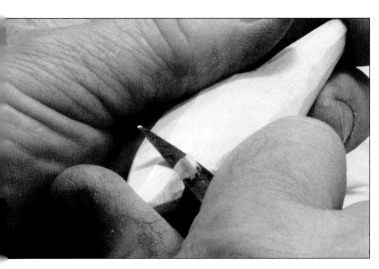

Carve and shape the entire nose of the lure. Remember when you remove wood from one side you must remove wood on the other side. Take a good look at the lure between cuts. This will help you to keep it symmetrical.

The bottom view.

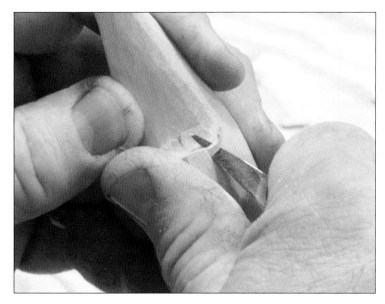

Now it is time to give the fin a pointed look. Slant your knife a little and, starting at the base of the fin, whittle out a little half-circle bevel, ending at the tip of fin.

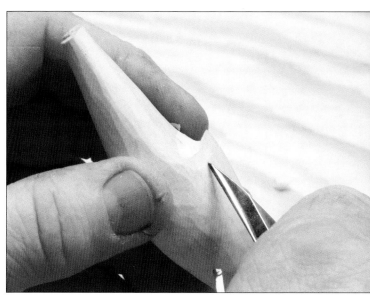

This is how the fin should look at this point.

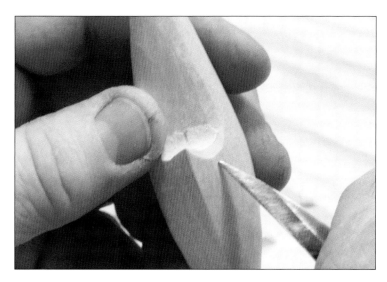

This is how the fin should look after you make this cut.

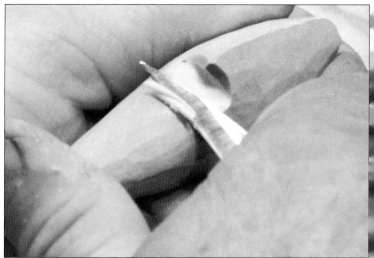

After shaping the fin you will need to blend the fin cuts into the tail of the lure as shown.

Do the same on the other side.

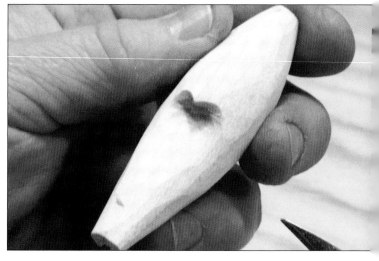

Top view of Pro Runner after fin has been carved.

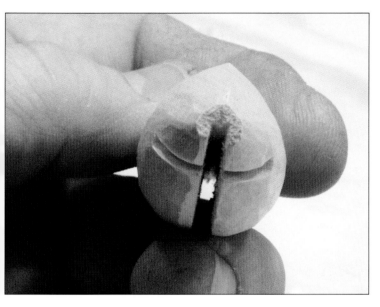

Front view of finished Pro Runner carving.

Bottom view.

Tail view.

Side view.

Top view.

Now that Pro Runner has been finish-carved it is time to sand and shape it.

I use 80 grit paper to bring Pro Runner to its final shape. I strongly suggest you use gloves for this task because the smoother the lure becomes the harder it is to hold on to it. The gloves that I use are excellent for this task.

Pro Runner should look like this after shaping.

Shape the entire nose.

Shape both sides of the fin.

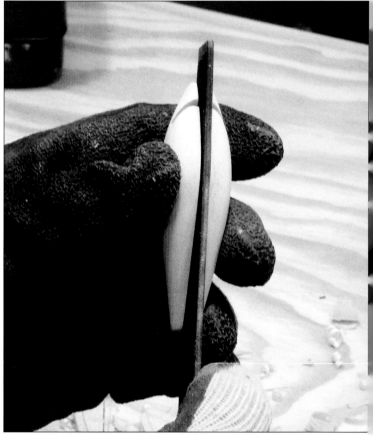

At this point you will need to clean up the dado in belly of the lure. For this task I use emery boards.

Shape the entire tail of the lure.

Change to a 400 grit paper and sand the entire lure. This makes a beautiful, smooth surface.

The wire rigging will be placed in the dado, and this 1/8" basswood filler will hold it in position.

Top view after sanding and shaping.

Dry fit the filler in lure.

Right side view.

View of the filler fit at nose of the lure.

Left side view.

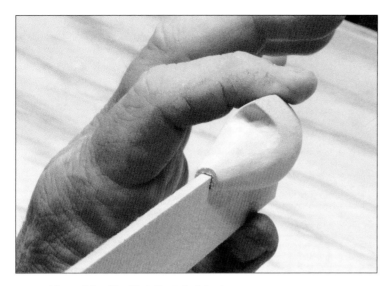

View of the filler fit at the tail of the lure.

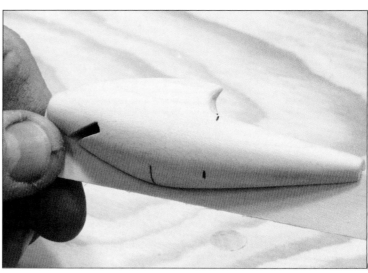

Your lure should look like this at this point. You should have the mark where the wire rig will exit the bottom of the lure and the mark for the cut line.

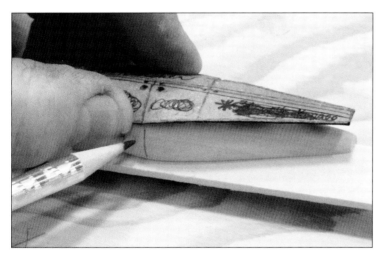

With the lure filler still inserted in the body of the lure mark the reference lines. Place the cardboard pattern on the lure. Mark a line to indicate where the wire rigging will exit the belly of the lure.

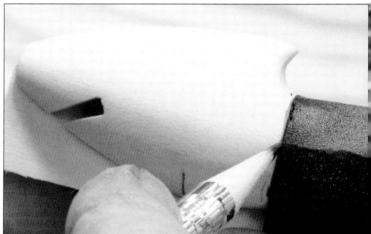

I use a piece of sandpaper to carry the cut line around the body, because you can fold it around the lure in a straight line. Mark in this line.

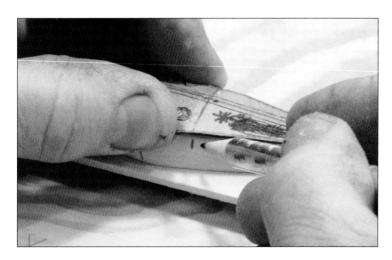

Mark the reference line that indicates where the lure will be cut into two parts.

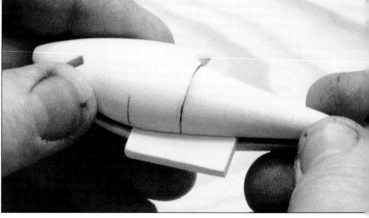

Take a piece of the 1/8" filler and insert it into the lure body at the location where the lure will be cut in two. This will keep the lure from tearing out when the blade exits the lure.

Saw the lure in two at the scroll saw.

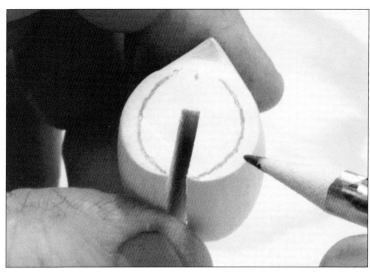

Do the same on the face of the nose portion of the lure.

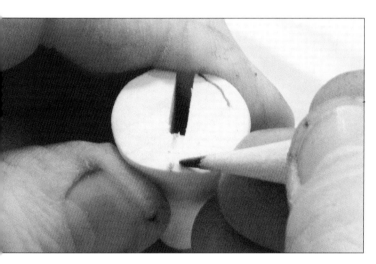

Lightly sand the edges after you have cut the lure in two, then draw some reference lines on the face of the tail piece on both sides. The "face" is the portion where the lure was cut in two.

With your knife slanted slightly carve away wood, beveling up to the lines on both sides.

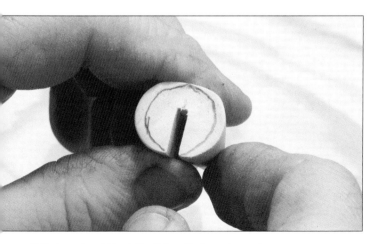

Tail piece should look like this with lines drawn in.

The nose portion of the lure should look like this after lines have been cut away.

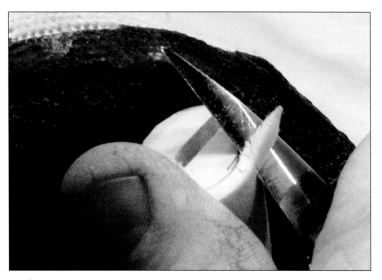

Do the same on the tail portion of lure.

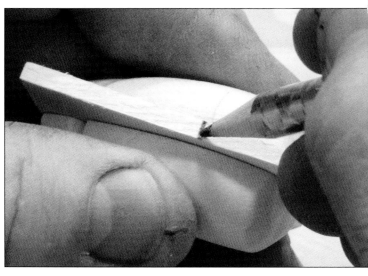

Insert filler into the front half of lure body.

This is what both halves of the lure should look like at this point. The purpose of these cuts is to give the lure its swimming action in the water.

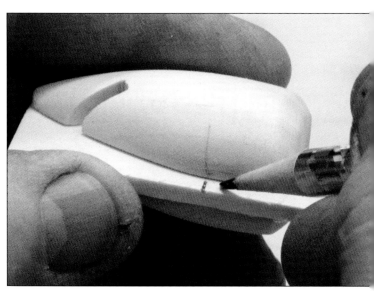

Mark the location on the bottom edge of the filler where the wire rigging will exit the lure body.

Sand both sections of the lure smooth.

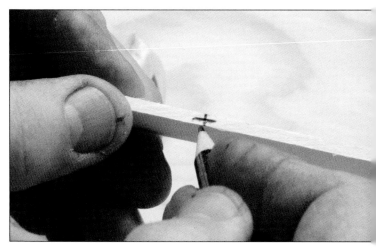

Mark a center line at this location on the edge of the filler about 3/16" long. The center of this mark and both ends will be drilled. This will center both lines.

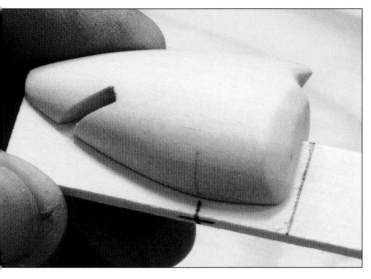

Insert the filler back into the lure body and mark the line where filler is to be cut in two. Cut filler to correct length.

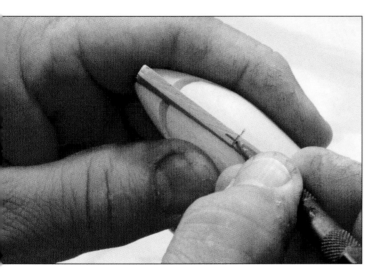

Use a nailset to make a small hole at the center mark on the bottom edge of filler. You do this so your drill bit will not drift to one side when you begin to drill the 1/16" diameter hole through filler.

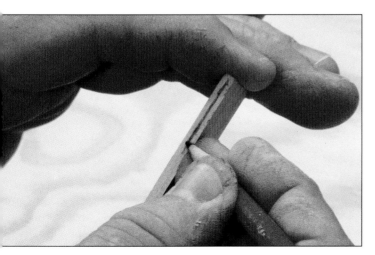

Flip the filler over and using your middle finger as a guide to draw in a center line the full length of the top edge of filler. This will be sawed out later and I will cover it in detail.

At the drill press we will drill the filler where the rigging will be. First of all, check all the adjustments on your drill press. Make sure your drill table is at zero and is level side to side. Make some practice holes to be sure your drill press is drilling straight. Second you need to make a block like the one that I am using. It is just a block of wood with 90 degree square cut from one side, and is used to support the filler block while it is being drilled. You can view this in the section of this book called jigs and rigs. Now hold the filler tight in the groove of the block with the bottom edge up, align the bit with the center point, and drill the 1/16" hole all the way through the filler.

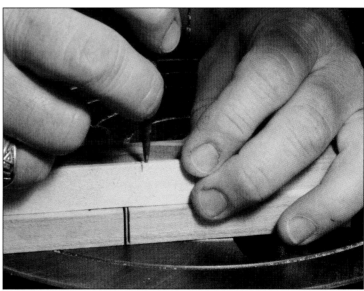

After you have drilled the first hole use the nailset to make a depression at each end of the mark made earlier. One depression will be on each side of the first hole drilled.

Use these depressions to align the drill bit and drill both of these holes all the way through the filler. This is the beginning of a slot for the wire rigging.

Place the filler block in a hobby vise with the top side up, revealing the center line that you made. At this point you can see the slot that was just cut for the wire rig. It is centered on the line.

At this point I use a small cylinder shaped diamond tip bit. I lower the bit into the center hole and slide the filler block from side to side to remove the wood between the holes that I drilled. This will give you a perfect slot in filler. Turn filler over and do the same from the other side.

For this step I suggest that you purchase one of these little saw bits. You can get one at your local hardware store. This little saw makes for a quick and beautiful cut. For this task I use my power carver, but if you don't have a power carver you can use a Dremel tool. Take the little saw and saw out the line down the center of the filler block, creating a channel. Shorten the depth of the cut at the very end of the nose portion of the filler channel. This will fit the wire rigging firmly and securely in the nose of the lure.

Now take a riffler file and clean up the slot.

With an emery board, smooth up edges of filler block.

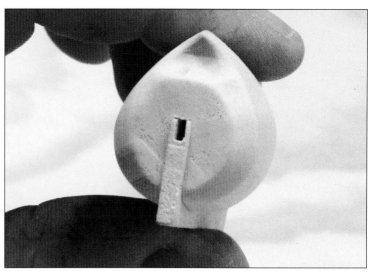

Now dry fit the filler into lure body to check for snuggness. This is the view from the back end of front of lure body. The fit is very good.

Clean out the channel with the emery board.

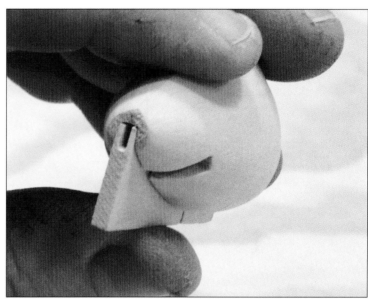

This is the view from the nose end. The fit here is excellent also, so let's move on.

The filler should look like this when finished.

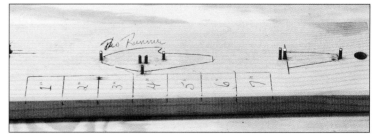

It is time to create a rigging board. Trace the Pro Runner Pattern onto a pine board. Trace the tail section on the board as a separate pattern. Refer back to the blueprint. Drive nails in at the locations where bends will take place in the wire rigging. Cut the nails off about a 1/4 inch above board. You can draw in a rule of measure on the board; this makes it quick and easy to measure wire when building a rig.

A close-up view of rig board. This rig is for upper body rigging. Sections are separated because we are making a broke back lure.

Start by laying the wire from the middle of the lure to the nail at the nose. This is where you make your first bend.

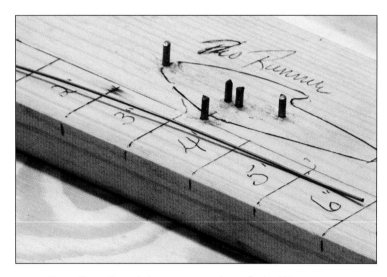

You will use the rule to measure a piece of wire 6" long.

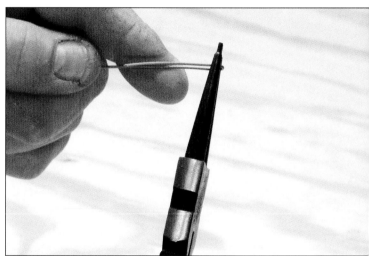

Take some round-nose pliers and make the first bend.

Cut the wire to 6" long. This should be a little more than you will need.

Place the wire back on rig board. It should look like this after first bend.

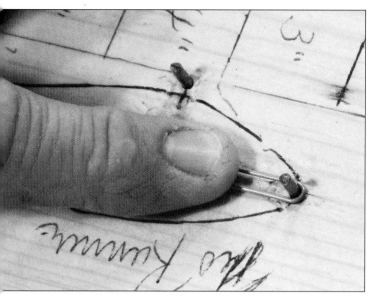

The fit should look like this at the nose of the lure.

Make the third bend at bottom of lure. Squeeze the wire to form an eye at the bottom. Bend the wire around the fourth nail.

Now take a pair of needle-nose pliers and squeeze wire around the nail to form an eye.

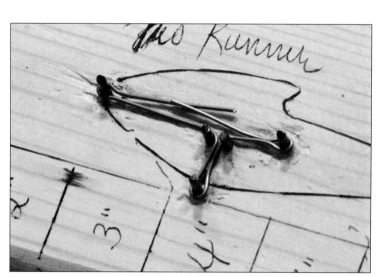

Finally bend the wire around the fifth nail. This will bring the wire back to the center of the lure. Squeeze the wire around the last nail to create an eye.

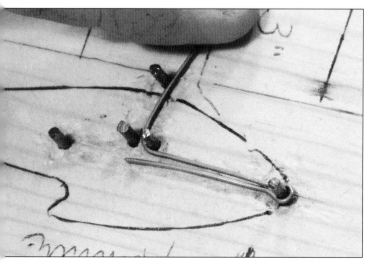

Now make a second bend at the next nail.

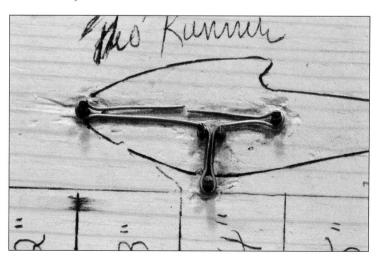

Now cut the wires so they meet in the center of the lure. The wire rigging for the upper lure body is complete.

Cut a piece of wire 4" long. This will be for the tail rigging.

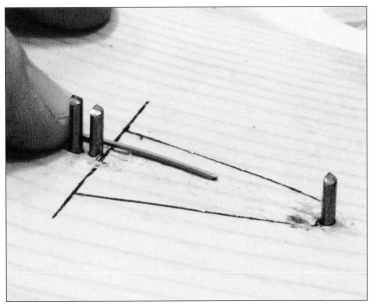

Place the wire so it extends to the middle of the tail section on the rigging jig. This marks the first bend.

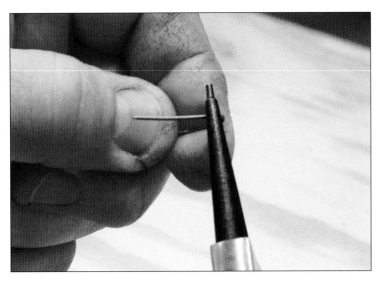

With the round nose pliers, make the first bend.

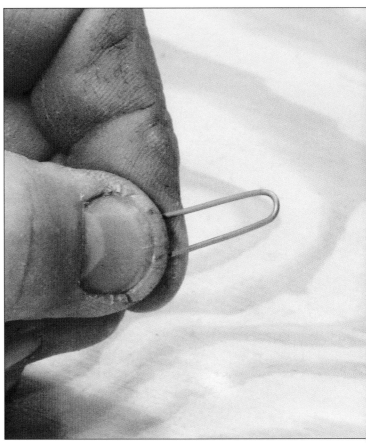

The bend should look like this.

Place the wire rig back on the board. The wire should look like this before further bending.

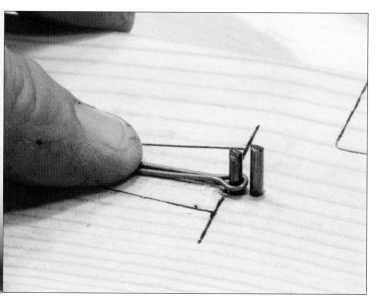

Squeeze wire around the nail for an eye.

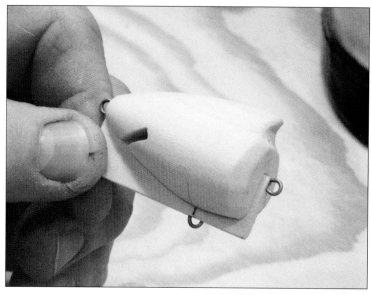

Now dry fit the lure rigging and filler block into upper body of the lure. This is a perfect fit.

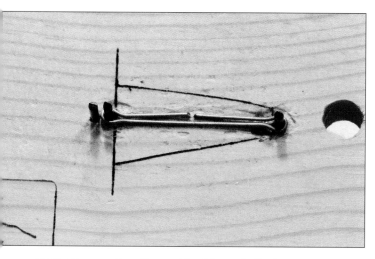

Do the same on the other end for this result. You have now completed both wire riggings that you will use in your lure.

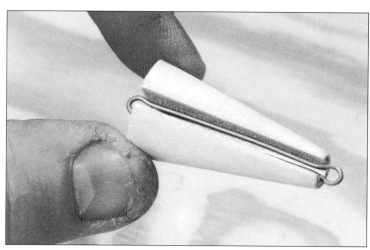

Check the wire rig fit in the tail section of the lure body. This is also a very good fit.

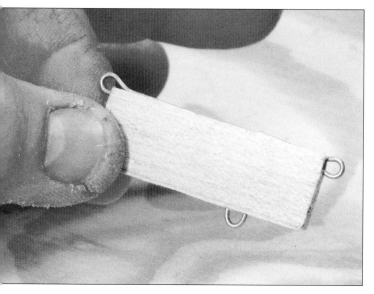

Dry fit the rigging into the filler block for the upper body.

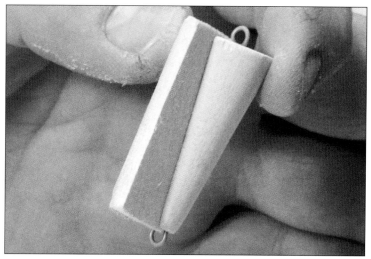

Cut a piece of filler stock to the length of the tail. No grooves are cut into this section. It will push in and press against the wire rig. If this fit is okay we are ready to assemble the lure.

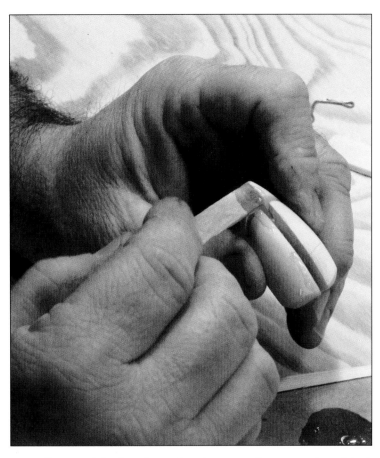

For assembling lures I use a two-ton epoxy. You can purchase this at your local hardware store. You may want to use latex gloves for this step. For the front section I squeeze out enough epoxy to form a half-dollar-size circle. Mix the epoxy thoroughly. Fill the dado in lure body with epoxy. I do this with a popsicle stick that I have trimmed to a paddle shape on the end.

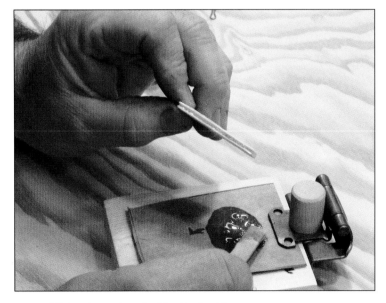

Fill the channel on the filler block with epoxy.

Apply epoxy to one side of the filler block.

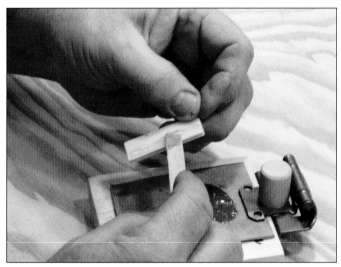

Do the same on the other side of the filler block.

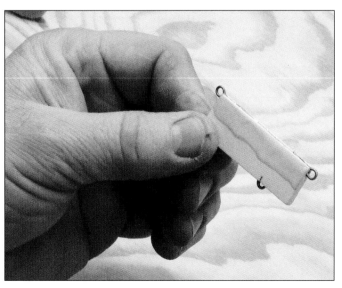

Insert wire rigging into the filler block.

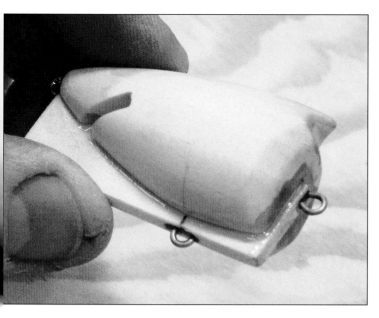

Insert the filler block and rigging into the belly of the lure. Wipe off any excess epoxy that comes out of dado.

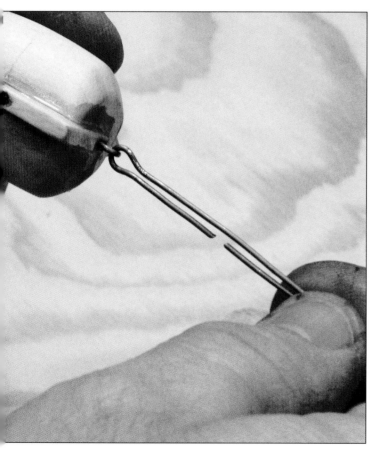

Now take the wire rigging for the tail section of the lure and hook it through the eye of the front half of lure.

Place wire rigging into tail section.

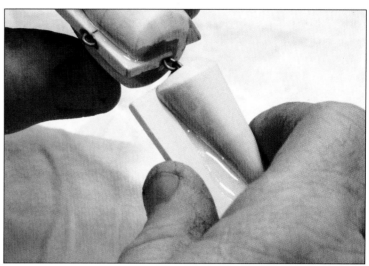

Coat filler block for the tail section with epoxy on both sides. Press the filler block into place. Wipe off excess epoxy, including at swivel joint between the lure halves.

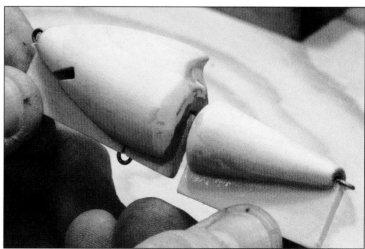

This is how the Pro Runner should look after all pieces are fitted.

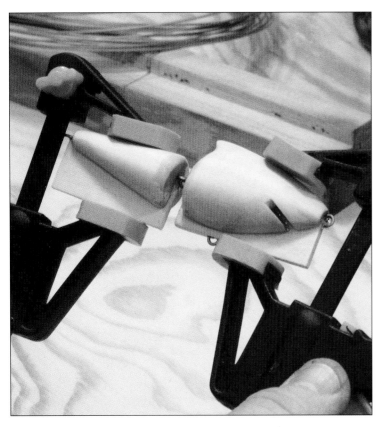

Clamp the fillers in place. Only light pressure is needed. Let the Pro Runner dry for about 2 to 3 hours at room temperature before proceeding.

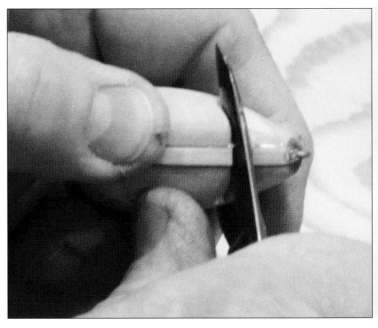

Cut out the filler block in the lip slot.

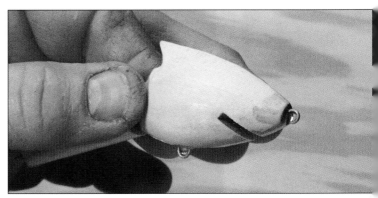

When the filler is cleaned out at lip slot you will be able to see the bottom edge of the wire rigging. Just clean around it.

After the lure has dried, trim off any excess body filler. Trim down close to belly of lure but not all the way. We will sand down the last bit to create a smooth surface.

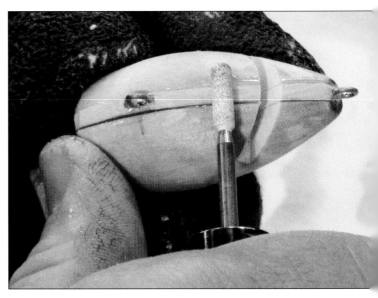

Now I use a cylinder-shaped bit to sand the filler block until it is nearly flush with the lure body.

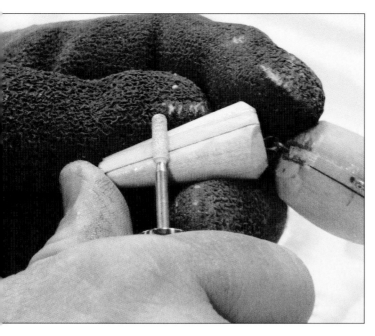

Do the same on the tail section of the lure.

I use the little cylinder-shaped diamond bit to clean epoxy from the lip slot.

I change to a smaller cylinder-shaped bit and sand around the eye in the nose of the lure.

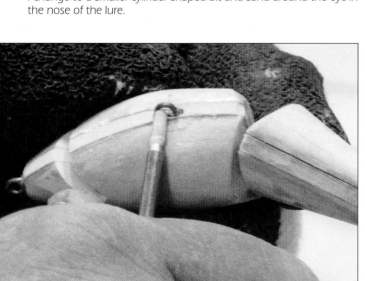

I use the same bit to sand around the eye in the belly of the lure.

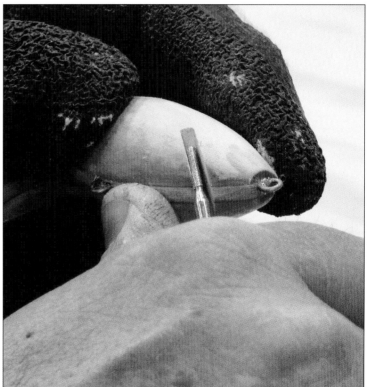

Clean all the epoxy from the top, bottom, and sides of the lip slot.

Now take a riffler file and dress up the lip slot.

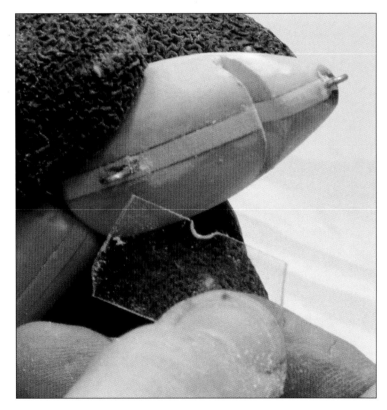

While dressing up the lip slot with the file, periodically test fit a piece of scrap acrylic, adjusting the lip slot to get a good fit.

The lip should fit like this when finished. You want a snug fit, not a loose one.

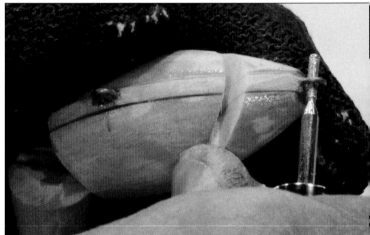

Use the same cylinder-shaped diamond bit to clean epoxy from all the eyes in the lure's rigging.

This is how the Pro Runner should look at this point, after cleaning out the eyes and the swivel joint.

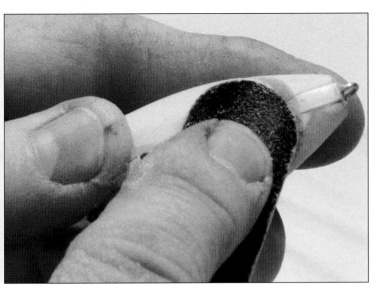

Use emery board to sand the filler block down flush with the lure body.

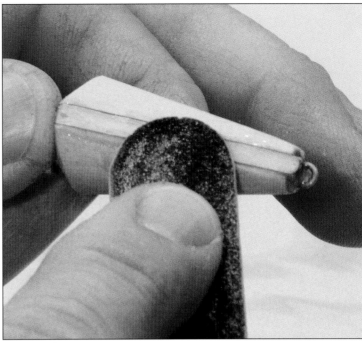

Use the emery board to sand the tail section in the same way.

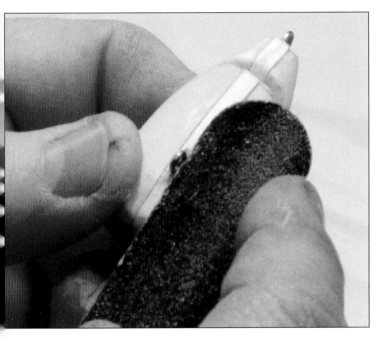

The emery board allows you to sand right up to the eyelets.

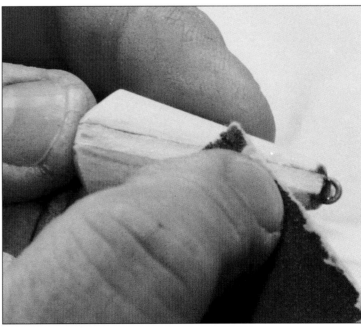

Go back to the 80 grit paper to define and blend the shape.

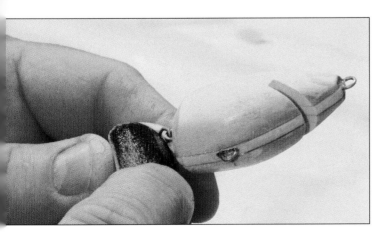

Use the emery board to sand between the two lure halves.

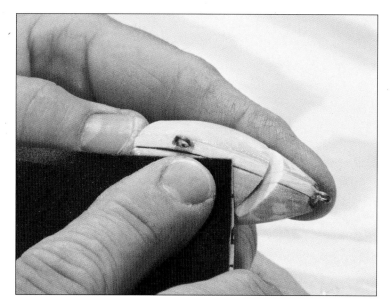

Finally use 400 grit paper to complete the final sanding of the lure.

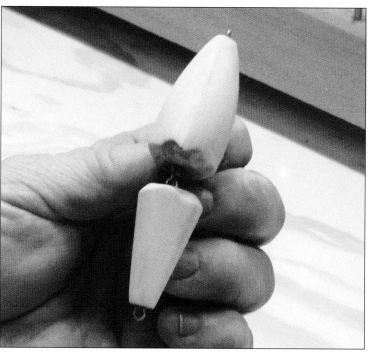

Top view.

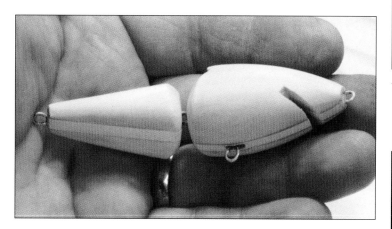

The Pro Runner after final sanding. Side view.

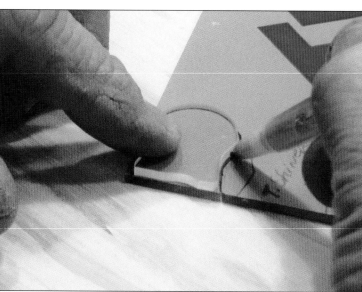

Now it is time to create a lip for the Pro Runner. Refer back to the blueprint for the pattern of the lip. Trace this shape onto a piece of 3/32" thick acrylic. You can purchase the acrylic from your local hardware store. For this step I use a scroll saw.

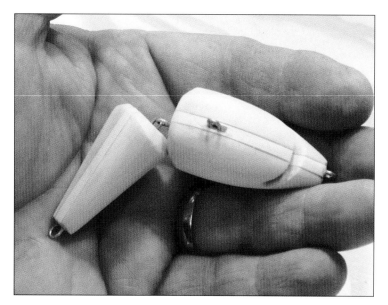

Bottom view.

This is the lip after it has been cut out.

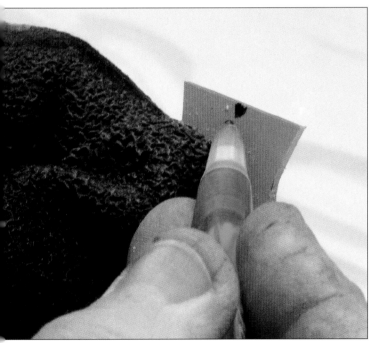

Put a mark at the center of the lip edge. This is the location where the lip will come into contact with the wire rig in the lure body.

Use the little cylinder-shaped diamond bit and begin cutting out the mark.

The lip should look like this.

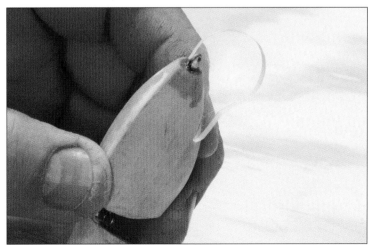

Remove the protective cover from the acrylic and dry fit the lip into the lure.

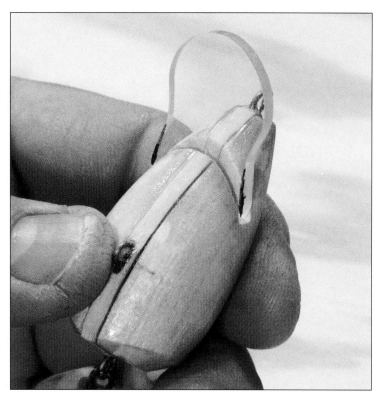

Center the lip with the lure. Take a permanent marker and mark areas that will need to be removed for a perfect fit. Because no two lures will be exactly the same, I use a standard lip pattern that will be close but not exact. With only minor modifications, this standard lip pattern can be made to work on Pro Runner lures.

Place the lip into a hobby vise.

Carve away marks on both sides of the lip.

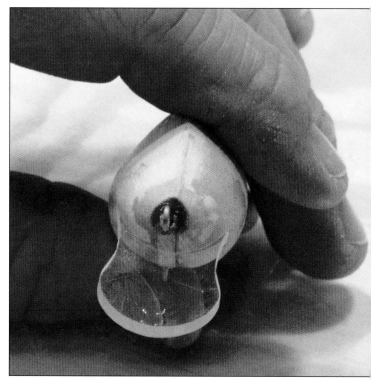

Insert the lip back into lure and check the fit. If the fit is good remove the lip and take it back to the vise. We will now dish out a spot on the lip to give it some action in the water and cause the lure to dive down when cranked in.

I use a ball-nosed bit to make a circle-shaped dip in the lip.

This is how the lip should look after grinding in the dish-shaped circle.

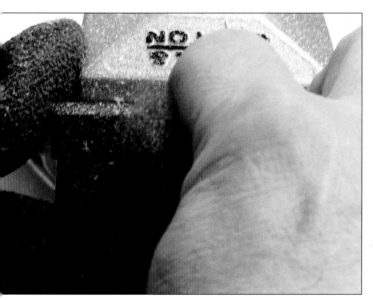

Take a piece of fine steel wool and polish the lip.

This is how the lip should look after polishing.

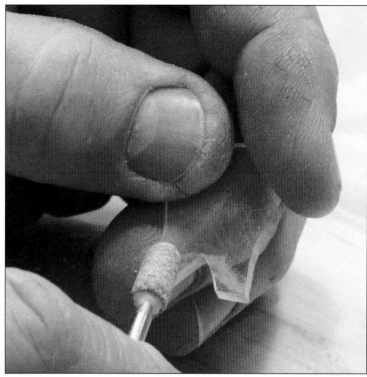

Now rough up the surface of the lip where it will be inserted into the lip slot.

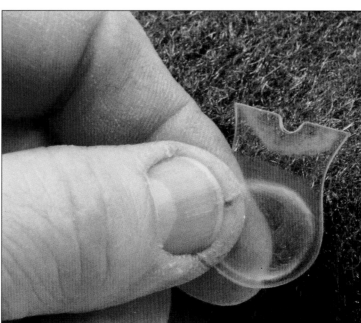

The lip should look like this before inserting into the lure.

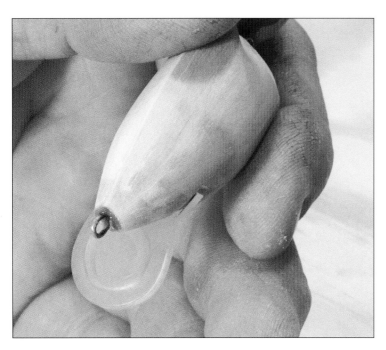

Check the fit once more before gluing the lip in place.

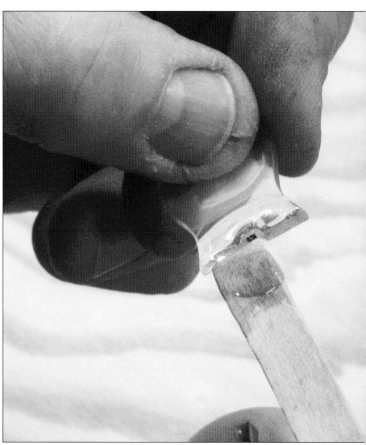

Apply epoxy to the lip as shown.

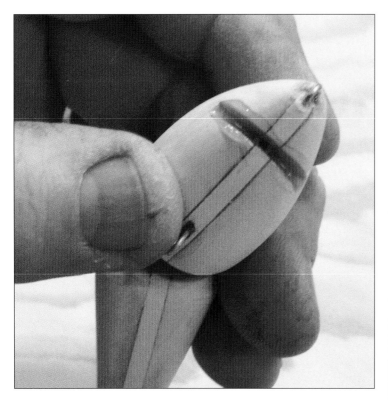

Apply epoxy to all surfaces in the lip slot.

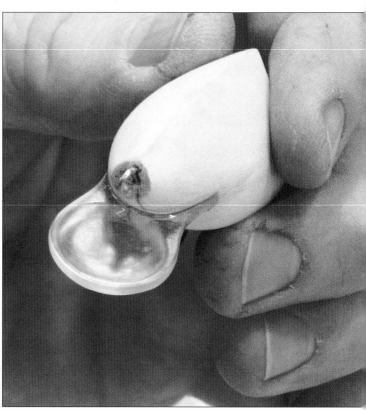

Set the lip in place.

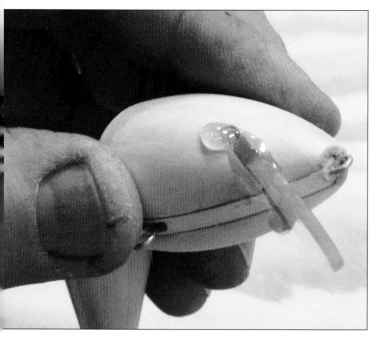

Wipe off any excess epoxy.

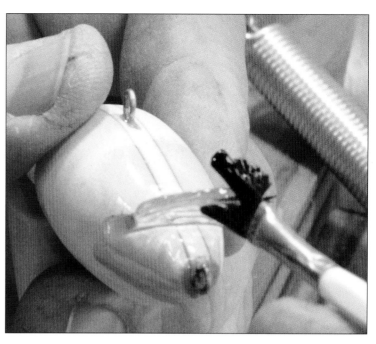

Squeeze out a circle of epoxy about the size of a half dollar. Mix the epoxy thoroughly. Apply epoxy around nose and at the lip before placing the lure in the epoxy jig.

At this point we are ready to apply the first coat of epoxy finish to the entire lure. I strongly suggest that you build an epoxy jig. Refer to the chapter of jigs and rigs where I have drawn plans for it.

Place the lure in epoxy jig and lock it down with the spring. From this point on you will not have to handle the lure until the epoxy dries. You can rotate the lure by turning the spring.

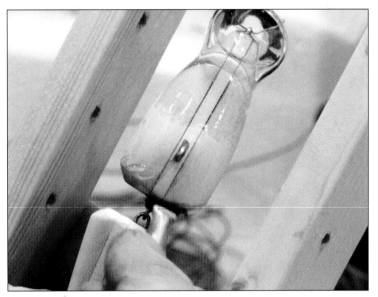

Apply epoxy to the surfaces between top and bottom lure bodies.

Apply epoxy to the entire surface of lure.

Bottom view of the lure after the first coat of epoxy.

Side view. Set lure aside for about 2 to 3 hours to dry.

After the first coat of epoxy has dried you will need to lightly sand the lure with 1000 grit paper.

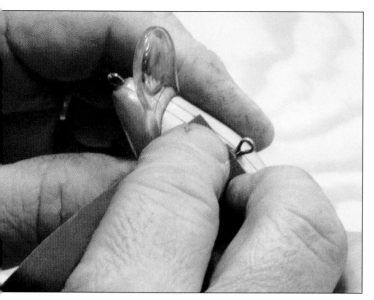

Sand the entire surface of the lure. This prepares the surface for painting and makes for a smooth, professional job. After sanding clean all the residue from the surface of the lure before painting. Let's paint.

Tape off the lip with paper tape and insert lure into paint stand.

At this point I strongly suggest that you build a paint stand. I have laid out a drawing for this stand in the jig and rig chapter. With this stand I can paint 5 lures at one time and I don't have to hunt down my paints. They are at hand's reach.

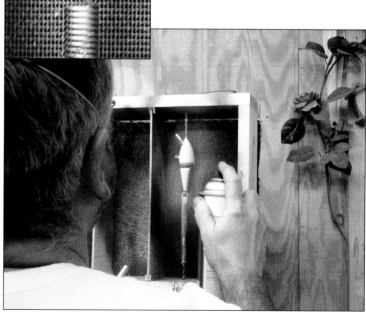

Lightly tint the entire lure with white paint and let this tack up.

The result.

Lightly paint back of lure orange. Let this tack up. Don't paint heavily at first or you will experience runs in paint.

After the lure has dried it is time to give him his name. I write this on the tail section of the lure.

This is the Pro Runner after the basic painting is complete.

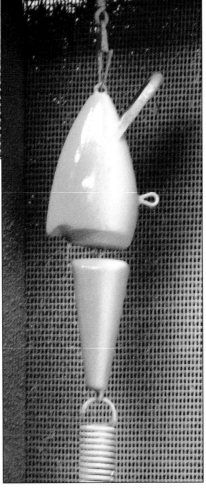

Now complete the painting of the orange on the lure back and the white on the belly of the lure. Now you can paint a light red tint on the nose to represent bleeding bait if you choose. Leave the lure in the paint stand to dry.

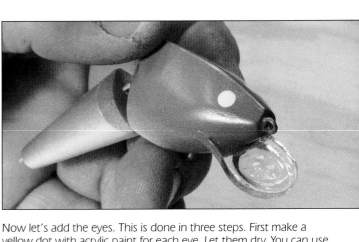

Now let's add the eyes. This is done in three steps. First make a yellow dot with acrylic paint for each eye. Let them dry. You can use a hair dryer to speed up this process.

Next add orange dots over the yellow ones. Make these a little smaller than the yellow ones. Let them dry.

Now add black dots that are a little smaller than the orange dots. Let them dry. The eyes are complete.

Add small black dots to the belly of the lure.

Like I told you before, the best thing about the epoxy jig is that the lure remains in the jig until finished. Now add large and small black dots to the entire surface of the lure. Rotate the lure by turning the spring.

Close-up of the lure with the painting complete.

Now apply the second coat of epoxy.

Let the lure dry in the epoxy stand for about 2 to 3 hours.

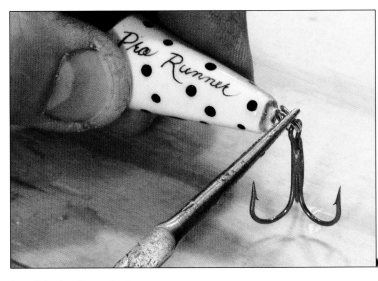

Install the hooks on the lure.

Now add the third and final coat of epoxy and let it dry.

Side view of the Pro Runner.

Back view of the Pro Runner.

Attach split rings to the hooks.

Congratulations you have just completed the Pro Runner lure.

Let's go fishing!

Ol' Ralphie's Lure Boxes

For all my boxes I use craft wood from my local hardware store, generally either pine or poplar. I purchase 1/4" x 2-1/2" x 2 feet long pieces. For this box we will use poplar. The box is composed of six pieces. Remember the length of the box is determined by the length of the Pro Runner lure. I find that 5-1/2" gives the right amount of space for the lure. You will need to cut 3 pieces to 5-1/2" long for the sides and bottom of the box. The lid piece will be cut to 5-3/4" long, so that when the lid is closed it will be flush with end piece. Cut the front end piece to measure 2-1/8" high x 2-3/4" long. Cut the back piece to measure 2-1/2" high x 2-3/4" long. These pieces will be a little long but this is okay. You will round these corners off at the sander. Set your table saw to cut a 1/8" deep dado along the top and bottom of the side pieces to accommodate the lid and the bottom piece.

Next, set the table saw fence at 1/4", then cut a dado down each edge of the sides.

Reset your table saw fence at 3/8", and cut a dado abutting the dado you have already cut. Do this on each side. These two cuts will produce 1/4" dados, 1/8" deep and running along the top and bottom edges of the side pieces, with a 1/8" reveal. You will need to clean out the dados with some sand paper.

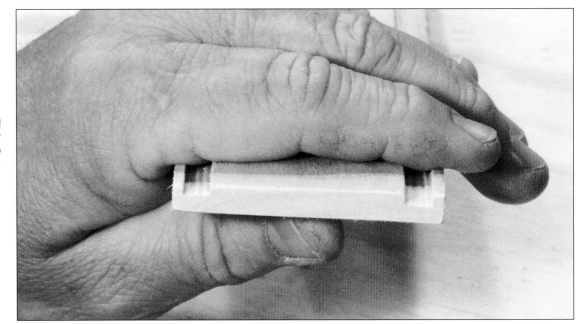

The side piece will look like this after you have cleaned up the dado.

Cut to the desired length. Both sides are ready for assembly. The end pieces do not require a dado cut.

Cut two pieces of 1/4" craft wood for the top and bottom of the box. Cut the bottom piece to the same length as the two side pieces as explained earily. Cut the lid of the box to measure 1/4" longer than the side and bottom pieces. This will allow for a 1/4" overlap at the front of the box. Dry fit pieces together as shown.

As I described earlier cut the top piece 1/4"
longer so it will be flush with front of box after
end pieces are glued on.

If everything looks good. We
are ready to glue the box.
Drill a hole 3/16" deep with a
3/8" Forstner bit at one end
of top piece for a wooden
button. This button
becomes a push-pull knob
for the lid.

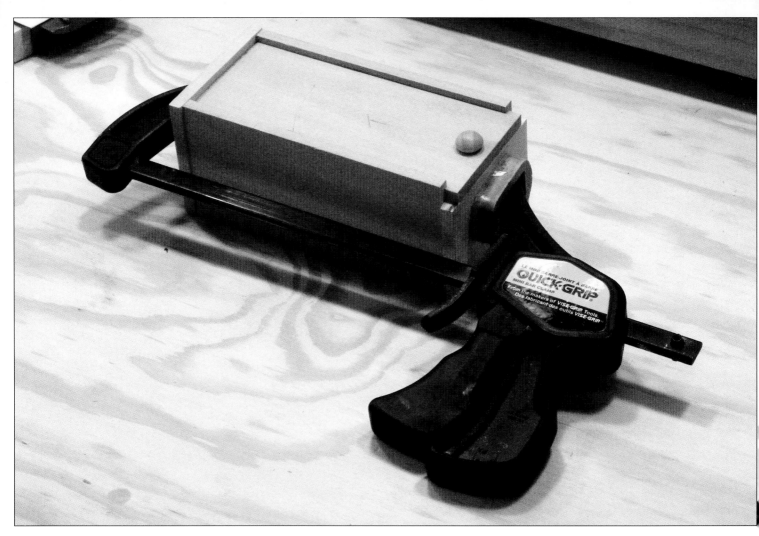

Apply glue to bottom dado joint and to each end piece. Do not apply glue to top dado. This is so lid can slide in and out. Clamp the box as shown and let it dry. After box has dried, round the corners of the box on the belt sander. Check that the top will slide in and out freely. You may need to sand dados just a little to get the proper slide action on the lid. Now is the time to autograph your box with a wood burner or however you please. When it is finished apply Linseed oil to the box. After the Linseed oil has dried I fill my boxes with shavings from my planer. I find this to be very appealing.

The finished box for Pro Runner.

Greg's Gallery

Pro Flex Shad

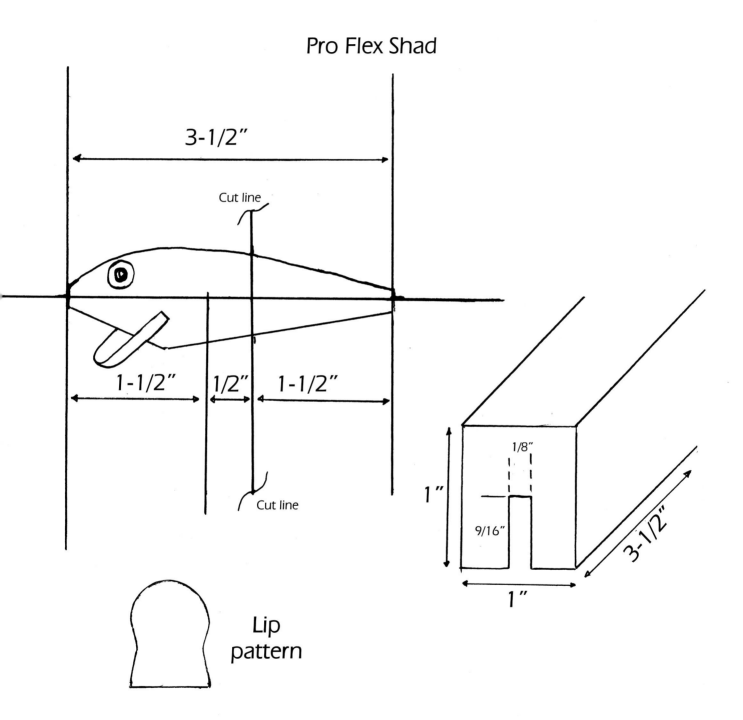

3-1/2"

Cut line

1-1/2" **1/2"** **1-1/2"**

Cut line

1/8"

1"

9/16"

3-1/2"

1"

Lip
pattern

The drawing for the "Pro Flex Shad" lure. This lure is made in essentially the same way, but is a solid body lure and a little smaller. With the basic skills you have learned in this book you can experiment with a variety of designs until you find the one that works for you! Happy fishing!